I0796267

Moby Dick

Lightbox Literature Studies

John Perritano

LIGHTBOX
openlightbox.com

Lightbox is an all-inclusive digital solution for the teaching and learning of curriculum topics in an original, groundbreaking way. Lightbox is based on National Curriculum Standards.

STANDARD FEATURES OF LIGHTBOX

AUDIO High-quality narration using text-to-speech system

VIDEOS Embedded high-definition video clips

ACTIVITIES Printable PDFs that can be emailed and graded

WEBLINKS Curated links to external, child-safe resources

SLIDESHOWS Pictorial overviews of key concepts

TRANSPARENCIES Step-by-step layering of maps, diagrams, charts, and timelines

INTERACTIVE MAPS Interactive maps and aerial satellite imagery

QUIZZES Ten multiple choice questions that are automatically graded and emailed for teacher assessment

KEY WORDS Matching key concepts to their definitions

MORE Extra information and details on the subject

FIRST HAND Letters, diaries, and other primary sources

DOCS Speeches, newspaper articles, and other historical documents

Contents

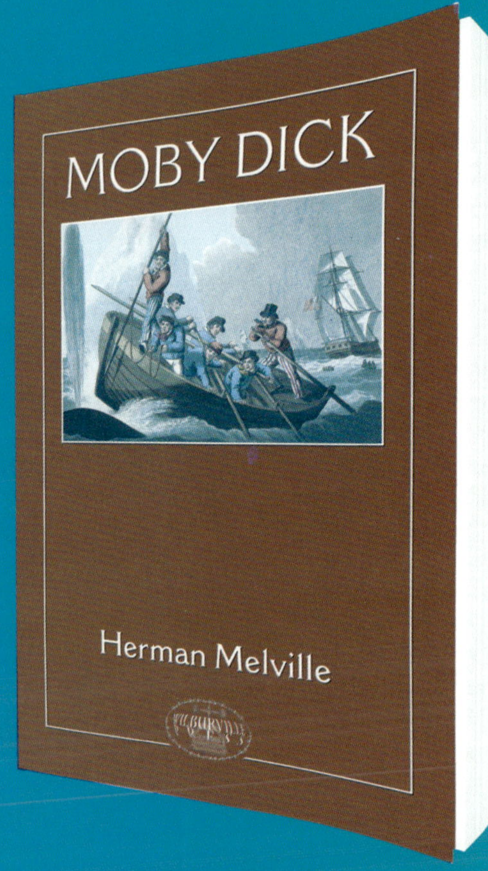

EXTENSION ACTIVITY

Researching for a Writing Assignment

Students will complete a thorough research process to prepare for a writing assignment, and organize their research in a logical manner that supports their writing. An exemplary research process will meet the following criteria.

- Creates a goal for the research, based on the topic and working thesis
- Creates specific, thoughtful, and inventive research questions that are relevant to the topic of the writing assignment
- Produces a list of categories, key words, and related ideas to effectively assist in researching
- Uses high-quality sources that pertain to the topic and come in a variety of formats, such as books, journals, primary sources, websites, and databases
- Determines accuracy of all sources
- Uses sources that provide balanced research and various perspectives on the topic in question
- Takes notes to highlight the key facts and ideas in order to answer all research questions
- Extracts relevant, detailed information from the sources during the note-taking process
- Organizes the research notes in a clear and concise manner
- Organizes the research notes logically and in a way that sets up the information and ideas for analysis and the writing process
- Analyzes the information and produces ideas and points to support the working thesis
- Uses an effective and suitable format to present all research
- Properly cites all sources used

Herman Melville

Author of *Moby Dick*
1819–1891

Herman Melville was born Herman Melvill on August 1, 1819, the third of eight children. His parents, Allan and Maria Gansevoort Melvill, were well connected in society in New York City. Young Herman did not seem to like this or to fit in, much to his parents' dismay. After his father died, Melville started working for the family business. It was about this time that the family changed the spelling of its surname to Melville. When the business went **bankrupt**, Melville went to work on a merchant ship. Later, he joined a whaling expedition. The journey took saw him sail the Atlantic Ocean and the southern part of the Pacific.

> "Let us speak, though we show all our faults and weaknesses,—for it is a sign of strength to be weak, to know it, and out with it,—not in [a] set way and ostentatiously, though, but incidentally and without premeditation.— But I am falling into my old foible—preaching."
>
> Herman Melville
>
> Letter to Nathaniel Hawthorne
> June 29, 1851

MAP OF NORTHEAST UNITED STATES

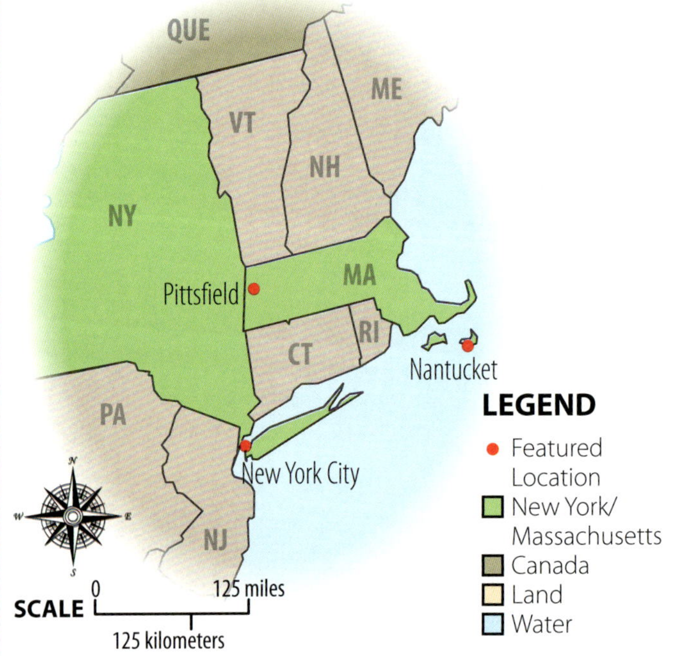

Melville's literary career began in 1846, when he published *Typee*, a story about his adventures in the South Seas. The novel was both a critical and financial success. The following year, *Omoo*, the sequel to *Typee*, was published. It, too, was well received. Melville continued to write, but his following works failed to live up to the popularity of *Typee* during his lifetime.

Melville idolized Nathaniel Hawthorne, the author of *The House of the Seven Gables* and *The Scarlet Letter*. When Melville was 31, he moved his family from New York City to the Berkshire Mountains in Massachusetts, where Hawthorne lived. Melville often confided to Hawthorne about his deepest feelings and anxieties, especially about his financial situation. "Though I wrote the Gospels in this century, I should die in the gutter," he once wrote to his friend.

In 1851, Melville published *Moby Dick,* a novel inspired by real-life events that occurred 30 years before. The *Essex*, a Nantucket whaling vessel helmed by 29-year-old Captain George Pollard Jr., was shipwrecked after being rammed by a sperm whale. In the aftermath of the attack, the surviving sailors suffered starvation and madness, before their eventual rescue 92 days later.

Herman Melville died on September 28, 1891, 40 years after *Moby Dick* was published. When *The New York Times* published Melville's obituary five days later, the paper **lamented** his death, saying, "There has died and been buried in this city during the current week, at an advance age, a man who is so little known, even by name, to the generation now in the vigor of life that only one newspaper contained an obituary of him, and this was about three or four lines." Although *Moby Dick* is now considered a masterpiece, the novel had sold only 3,715 copies at the time of Melville's passing.

TEACHER NOTES

Google Maps

780 Holmes Road, Pittsfield, Massachusetts

Use street view to explore Arrowhead, also known as the Herman Melville House, and its surrounding neighborhood. Today, Melville's former home is a museum.

Weblink

Amusing *Moby Dick* Rejection Letter Asks "Does It Have to Be a Whale?"

Examine a December 2016 article from *The Telegraph* highlighting a rejection letter Melville received.

1. Think about the editor's statements about the novel. Is there any merit to his analysis of Melville's manuscript? Are the publishing house's requests of Melville fair? Why or why not?
2. How different might the final novel have looked should Melville have heeded their requests? Compose a single-page description of the novel that imagines *Moby Dick* without its titular whale.

EXTENSION ACTIVITY

Holding a Classroom Debate

Students will form groups and prepare arguments for a debate on a controversial issue. Exemplary performance in a debate will meet the following criteria.

- Demonstrates in-depth understanding of the topic and related information
- Presents strong, logical, and convincing arguments
- Communicates in a clear and confident manner
- Maintains eye contact
- Uses clear vocal tone and a reasonable rate of vocal delivery
- Uses respectful and appropriate language and body language
- Delivers arguments, evidence, and counter-evidence in an engaging and persuasive manner
- Supports each major point of an argument with several relevant and detailed facts and examples
- Connects all arguments to the overall topic in a clear, concise, and organized manner
- Presents the arguments and supporting evidence in a clear, logical manner
- Presents clear, thorough, and accurate information throughout the debate
- Addresses all of the opposing team's arguments with counter-arguments
- Identifies any weakness in the opposing team's arguments
- Constructs strong and relevant counter-arguments using accurate information
- Presents strong and persuasive arguments throughout the debate
- Summarizes the arguments in the closing statement

Setting of the Novel

Most of the action in *Moby Dick* takes place aboard the *Pequod*, a whaling ship. It is on the *Pequod* that the book's narrator, Ishmael, recounts the story of Captain Ahab's hunt for the great leviathan, or whale. The ship, named after a Native American group from Connecticut, begins its three-year voyage in Nantucket, an island off the coast of Massachusetts. The ship was simply made, cheap to build, and home to about 35 sailors. Author Nathaniel Philbrick refers to the *Pequod* as "a mythic **incarnation** of America."

Snapshot

Whaling in Nineteenth Century Massachusetts

1807 Nantucket is home to 116 whaling vessels.

1843 The price of sperm whale oil is approximately $1.25 per gallon (3.78 liters).

1855 New Bedford is the port of 311 whaling vessels, and produces 1.3 million gallons of sperm whale oil.

Life Aboard Whaling Ships

"... take my word for it, you never saw such a rare old craft as this same rare old *Pequod*. She was a ship of the old school, rather small if anything; with an old-fashioned claw-footed look about her. Long seasoned and weather-stained in the typhoons and calms of all four oceans, her old hull's complexion was darkened like a French grenadier's, who has alike fought in Egypt and Siberia. Her venerable bows looked bearded. Her masts—cut somewhere on the coast of Japan, where her original ones were lost overboard in a gale—her masts stood stiffly up like the spines of the three old kings of Cologne. Her ancient decks were worn and wrinkled, like the pilgrim-worshipped flag-stone in Canterbury Cathedral where Becket bled. But to all these her old antiquities, were added new and marvelous features, pertaining to the wild business that for more than half a century she had followed."

Ishmael, Chapter 16

Whaling was big business in the nineteenth century, especially in New England. The sailors who hunted whales for oil often lived hard lives at sea. They would spend years aboard a whaling vessel, working and living among all types of people. Some sailors were new to whaling, while others were veteran whalers. The whale ship was an enclosed community, where the food served was often a revolting mix of greasy pork and hard biscuits. Ships were often filthy, oily, and smoky. Larger ships were able to go on longer voyages and required a larger crew. The longest whaling voyage is said to have lasted 11 years.

Although Ishmael does not spend much time in Nantucket, the whaling port is important to the events of *Moby Dick*. Many of the *Pequod*'s sailors are from Nantucket Island, which Ishmael describes as "an elbow of sand; all beach without a background." Today, Nantucket Island's year-round population is approximately 11,000. This figure can more than quadruple during the summer months due to an influx of vacationers and tourists.

TEACHER NOTES

Weblink

Life Aboard

Examine detailed descriptions of life aboard a whaling vessel on the New Bedford Whaling Museum website.

1. Compare and contrast the lives of a captain's mates with those of the foremast hands. How appealing does life aboard a whaling vessel in the 1800s sound for each? Why do you think people would choose this kind of career?
2. Research Bedford's other primary industry in the 1800s, and write a short composition comparing and contrasting its risks and rewards with that of living and working on a whaling vessel.

First Hand

Laura Jernegan: Girl on a Whaleship

Explore the pages of a journal kept by a six-year-old girl aboard a whaling vessel from 1868 to 1871.

1. What do Jernegan's journal entries suggest about the quality of life for a child on a whaling vessel? Besides Jernegan's youth, what other factors might contribute to the brevity of her daily entries?
2. How do you think children Jernegan's age would fare on a whaling vessel today? What struggles might they face? Defend your responses with clear reasoning.

EXTENSION ACTIVITY

Analyzing a Newspaper Article

Students will assess a newspaper article and write an analysis. An exemplary analysis will meet the following criteria.

- Identifies the topic of the article
- Identifies the main points and opinions presented in the article
- Identifies the writer of the article
- Presents information about the writer and infers how his or her life may have shaped this opinion
- Assesses the writer's reliability
- Analyzes how the writer makes his or her argument
- Uses evidence from the article to show how the writer supports his or her argument
- Analyzes the writer's use of literary devices to enhance the article
- Differentiates between the facts and opinions presented in the article
- Identifies when and where the article was published, and determines its intended audience
- Identifies and understands the goals of the article
- Assesses the effectiveness of the format (a newspaper opinion article) in presenting the writer's argument
- Connects the article to the societal and historical context in which it was written
- Infers what is not said about this topic in the article
- Identifies what information is unintentionally implied in the article
- Infers what other opinions may be presented about this topic and who may be most likely to express them
- Uses a number of other resources to analyze the context of the article

Time Period of the Novel

When Herman Melville wrote *Moby Dick*, the United States was pushing its way west and heading toward a civil conflict. Melville's novel came just before the end of the age of whaling. Whale oil was an important commodity for many years prior to the novel's publication. It was used mainly as a source of fuel, before discoveries of petroleum made whale oil obsolete. The oil was extracted from whale blubber through the process of boiling it, which took place aboard the ship. Melville details this process in Chapter 94.

Working with Whale Oil

"That whale of Stubb's, so dearly purchased, was duly brought to the *Pequod*'s side, where all those cutting and hoisting operations previously detailed, were regularly gone through, even to the baling of the Heidelburgh Tun, or Case.

While some were occupied with this latter duty, others were employed in dragging away the larger tubs, so soon as filled with the sperm [oil]; and when the proper time arrived, this same sperm [oil] was carefully manipulated ere going to the try-works, of which anon.

It had cooled and crystallized to such a degree, that when, with several others, I sat down before a large Constantine's bath of it, I found it strangely concreted into lumps, here and there rolling about in the liquid part. It was our business to squeeze these lumps back into fluid. A sweet and unctuous duty! No wonder that in old times this sperm [oil] was such a favourite cosmetic."

Ishmael, Chapter 94

Spermaceti is a wax-like substance found in the spermaceti organ of a sperm whale's head. Sperm whales are named for this organ as well. Spermaceti was the most prized of all types of whale oil, as it was used for fuel in oil lamps, as well as to produce cosmetics, lubricants, and a variety of other products.

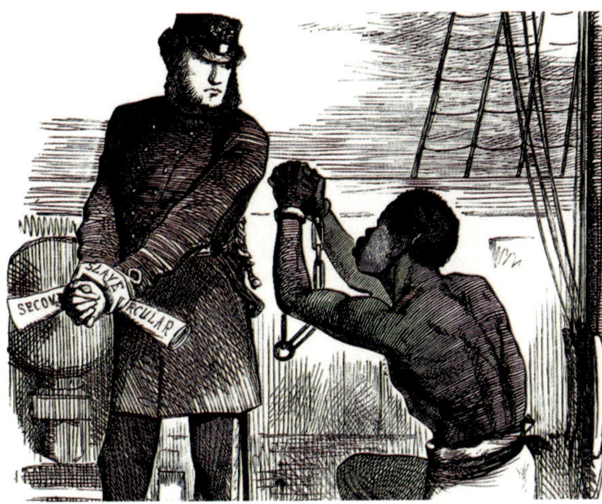

When Melville began writing *Moby Dick*, the United States was simmering in racial **prejudice** and regional animosity due to slavery. Slavery played a role in the economy of the southern states as the nation grew. It had been a divisive issue since the signing of the Declaration of Independence. By the time *Moby Dick* was published, the northern states had abolished slavery, and **abolitionists** were working to end slavery across the country.

The Fugitive Slave Act of 1850 unraveled years of peace stitched together by political compromise. This law required that escaped slaves be handed over to their owners no matter where they were found. This included the northern states, where slavery had been abolished. Tensions grew, and violence bubbled to the surface, threatening to split the nation. This conflict led in part to the outbreak of the U.S. Civil War in 1861, 10 years after *Moby Dick* was published.

TEACHER NOTES

Video

Moby-Dick the Massive White Sperm Whale

Analyze the first-hand experience of a whaler with a sperm whale in this documentary film clip.

1. What impression do you have of sperm whales after hearing the former whaler's story? In your opinion, was the whale attack provoked? Why or why not?
2. What reasons might a sperm whale have for ramming a boat? How might humans be misunderstanding the behavior of sperm whales?

Document

A Freeman's Resolve

Examine the article published in the October 18, 1950 edition of *The Anti-Slavery Bugle*.

1. How justified are the writer's intentions? Is it ever ethical to break the law? Why or why not?
2. How would you respond to a fugitive slave's request for shelter today? What considerations might factor into your decision?

EXTENSION ACTIVITY

Writing a Short Story

Students will choose an excerpt from the novel and use it as their inspiration in writing a short story. An exemplary short story will meet the following criteria.

- Engages the reader from the opening line
- Establishes a clear, consistent point of view
- Introduces a narrator and a setting
- Develops an engaging conflict at the heart of the narrative to build tension and keep the reader interested
- Develops characters and events through purposeful and well-crafted literary devices
- Creates a logical progression of events in the narrative that build upon each other using various techniques
- Explores ideas, concepts, and writing styles with creativity and originality
- Demonstrates a high level of skill in using appropriate narrative techniques to tell the story
- Concludes the narrative in a thoughtful, effective manner appropriate to the narrative
- Uses varied, purposeful diction and syntax to affect style and serve the narrative
- Writes with clarity, imagination, and a unique, personal voice
- Does not use stereotypes or clichés
- Uses effective, believable dialogue
- Uses correct spelling, grammar, and punctuation

Conflict in the Novel

Conflict in literature is a struggle between two or more opposing forces. When those forces come together, it creates tension that must be resolved. This struggle is often between the protagonist and antagonist, but there are other types of conflict found in literature, too. Conflict is a vital element of stories.

The Four Major Types of Conflict in Literature

MAN vs. MAN

The protagonist struggles against an opposing character, usually the antagonist. This is a common type of conflict in fiction, and generally features the fight between good and evil. In *The Wizard of Oz*, Dorothy struggles against the Wicked Witch of the West, who is determined to stop Dorothy and her friends from getting to the city of Oz.

MAN vs. SELF

The protagonist fights an inner battle. This struggle often involves a major decision that he or she must make. In *Star Wars Episode III: Revenge of the Sith*, young Anakin Skywalker must decide if he will serve the powers of good or evil. As the film unfolds, Anakin's choices shape and ultimately reveal his true character.

MAN vs. SOCIETY

The protagonist opposes the principles or actions of his or her society. This conflict is based upon the protagonist's beliefs or morals. In *The Hunger Games* series by Suzanne Collins, Katniss Everdeen volunteers to take her sister's place in a fight to the death called the Hunger Games. As the story progresses, Katniss gains the courage to stand against the tyrannical and oppressive Capitol that holds the Games.

MAN vs. NATURE

The protagonist faces an obstacle in nature. This may be an entire landscape or a symbolic representation of nature, such as an animal or natural disaster. In Ernest Hemingway's *The Old Man and the Sea*, an old fisherman struggles to reel in a giant fish—the greatest catch of his life.

Types of Conflict in *Moby Dick*

The two main types of conflict in *Moby Dick* are man versus self and man versus nature. Each of these conflicts plays a major role in the story.

Man versus Self

"Small reason was there to doubt, then, that ever since that almost fatal encounter, Ahab had cherished a wild vindictiveness against the whale, all the more fell for that in his frantic morbidness he at last came to identify with him, not only all his bodily woes, but all his intellectual and spiritual exasperations. The White Whale swam before him as the monomaniac incarnation of all those malicious agencies which some deep men feel eating in them, till they are left living on with half a heart and half a lung. . . . All that most maddens and torments; all that stirs up the lees of things; all truth with malice in it; all that cracks the sinews and cakes the brain; all the subtle demonisms of life and thought; all evil, to crazy Ahab, were visibly personified, and made practically assailable in Moby Dick."

Ishmael, Chapter 41

Man versus Nature

"'Aye, aye! It was that accursed white whale that razed me; made a poor pegging lubber of me for ever and a day!' Then tossing both arms, with measureless imprecations he shouted out: 'Aye, aye! and I'll chase him round Good Hope, and round the Horn, and round the Norway Maelstrom, and round perdition's flames before I give him up. And this is what ye have shipped for, men! To chase that white whale on both sides of land, and over all sides of earth, till he spouts black blood and rolls fin out.'"

Captain Ahab, Chapter 36

TEACHER NOTES

More

The Types of Conflict in *Moby Dick*

Analyze the excerpts from the novel revealing the types of conflict as they appear in *Moby Dick*.

1. How do these excerpts of conflict reveal the novel's theme? How do they reveal character? Explain and defend your ideas.
2. Write an analysis of Melville's development of conflict between Captain Ahab and Ishmael. What deeper truths may be suggested about these characters as a result of their conflict?

Weblink

What Is a Story?: Conflict—The Foundation of Storytelling

Examine the *Script* article about conflict in literature.

1. What makes Captain Ahab unique in the way he handles conflict? How do the other characters in the story create conflict for him? Conversely, how does Captain Ahab create conflict for the other characters in *Moby Dick*?
2. How does Captain Ahab respond to the "fight or flight" aspect of conflict? In what ways does this change throughout the novel? Defend your responses with evidence from the novel.

EXTENSION ACTIVITY

Analyzing a Video

Students will watch and assess a video related to a component of the novel, and write an analysis of the video. An exemplary video analysis will meet the following criteria.

- Identifies the purpose of the video
- Identifies the intended audience of the video
- Describes how the content of the video is presented
- Summarizes the information and opinions presented in the video
- Analyzes the quality of the content presented in the video
- Assesses the effectiveness of the video
- Discusses the technical aspects of the video and whether or not these enhance the content
- Determines whether the images and graphics used in the video relate to the content
- Determines whether the video is easy to follow and understand
- Gives the analysis a clear and consistent purpose
- Organizes the analysis in a logical, effective manner
- Presents a strong, clear argument about the video
- Provides strong and accurate details to support the argument about the video
- Considers other perspectives on the purpose and effectiveness of the video
- Makes connections between the video and the novel
- Properly integrates quotations from the video
- Cites all sources used in the analysis

Introducing the Characters

Characterization is crucial to effective story writing. Writers develop their characters to drive and serve their stories through one of two methods. In the direct method of characterization, the narrator relays descriptions of the character's important personality traits directly to the reader. In the indirect method, writers reveal personality traits indirectly through a character's dialogue, thoughts, and actions, as well as through the thoughts and dialogue of other characters. Ishmael is the narrator of *Moby Dick*, yet he does not directly tell readers much about himself. He does, however, tell us a great deal about the others in the novel.

Major Characters in *Moby Dick*

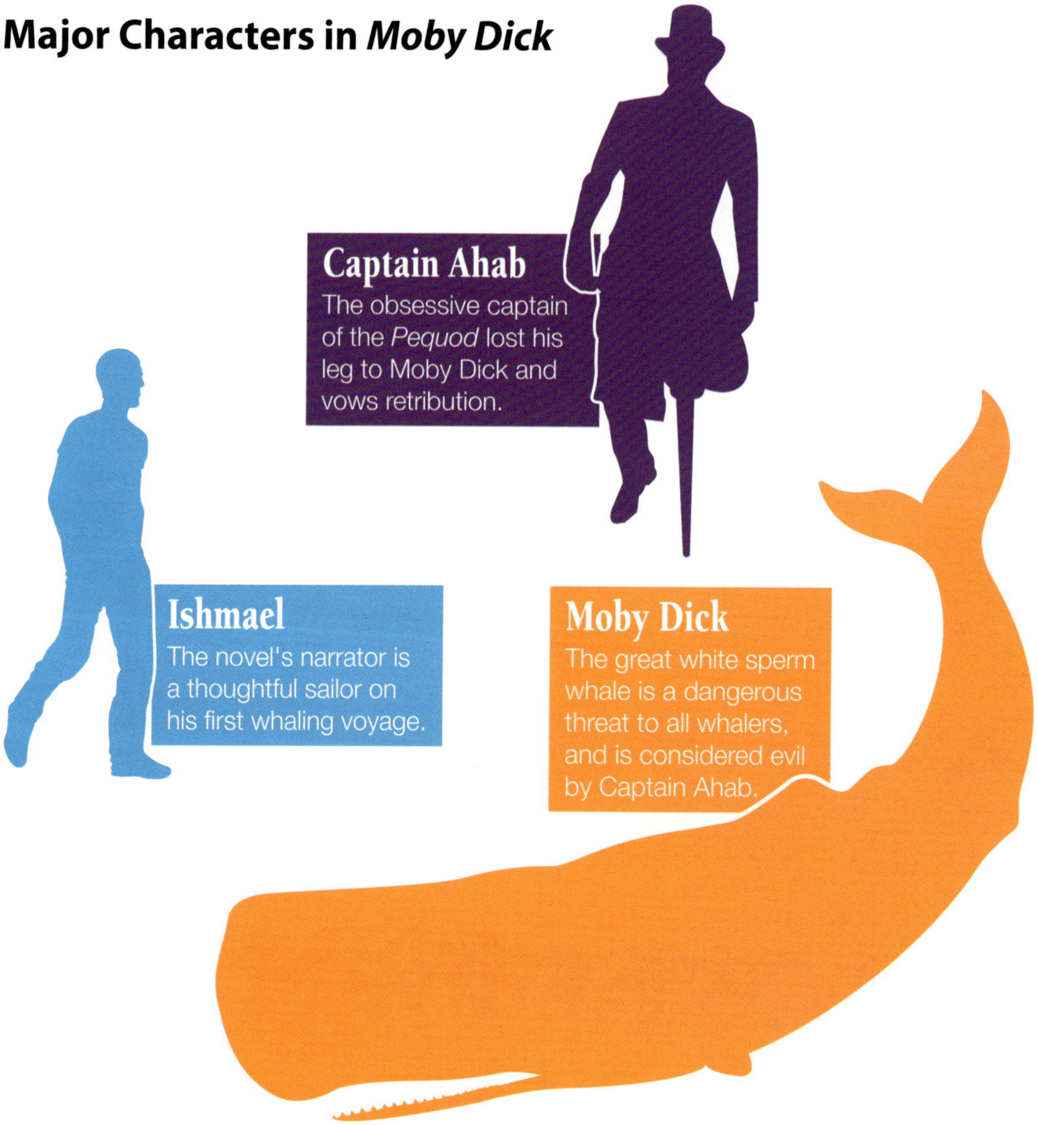

Captain Ahab
The obsessive captain of the *Pequod* lost his leg to Moby Dick and vows retribution.

Ishmael
The novel's narrator is a thoughtful sailor on his first whaling voyage.

Moby Dick
The great white sperm whale is a dangerous threat to all whalers, and is considered evil by Captain Ahab.

An argument can be made that both Captain Ahab and Moby Dick alternately play the role of both protagonist and antagonist at different times in the novel. Ahab is obsessive, overconfident, and brimming with **hubris**. He considers Moby Dick the embodiment of evil. However, it can be argued that Ahab is the evil antagonist, as he constantly puts his crew in danger in his relentless pursuit of revenge.

Moby Dick is portrayed with intelligence, boldness, and other human-like characteristics. He flees from whalers, only to return again. Moby Dick uses the whalers' own tools to slay them. He also seems to have an almost mythical quality, as he supposedly appears in several locations at the same time.

The other characters in *Moby Dick* are similarly portrayed in vivid fashion, such as Queequeg, the tattooed harpooner from Polynesia. Another major character is Starbuck, who sees Ahab's plan for what it is, and opposes it from the start. Where Ahab is depicted as **maniacal** and **bombastic**, Starbuck is calm and reasonable.

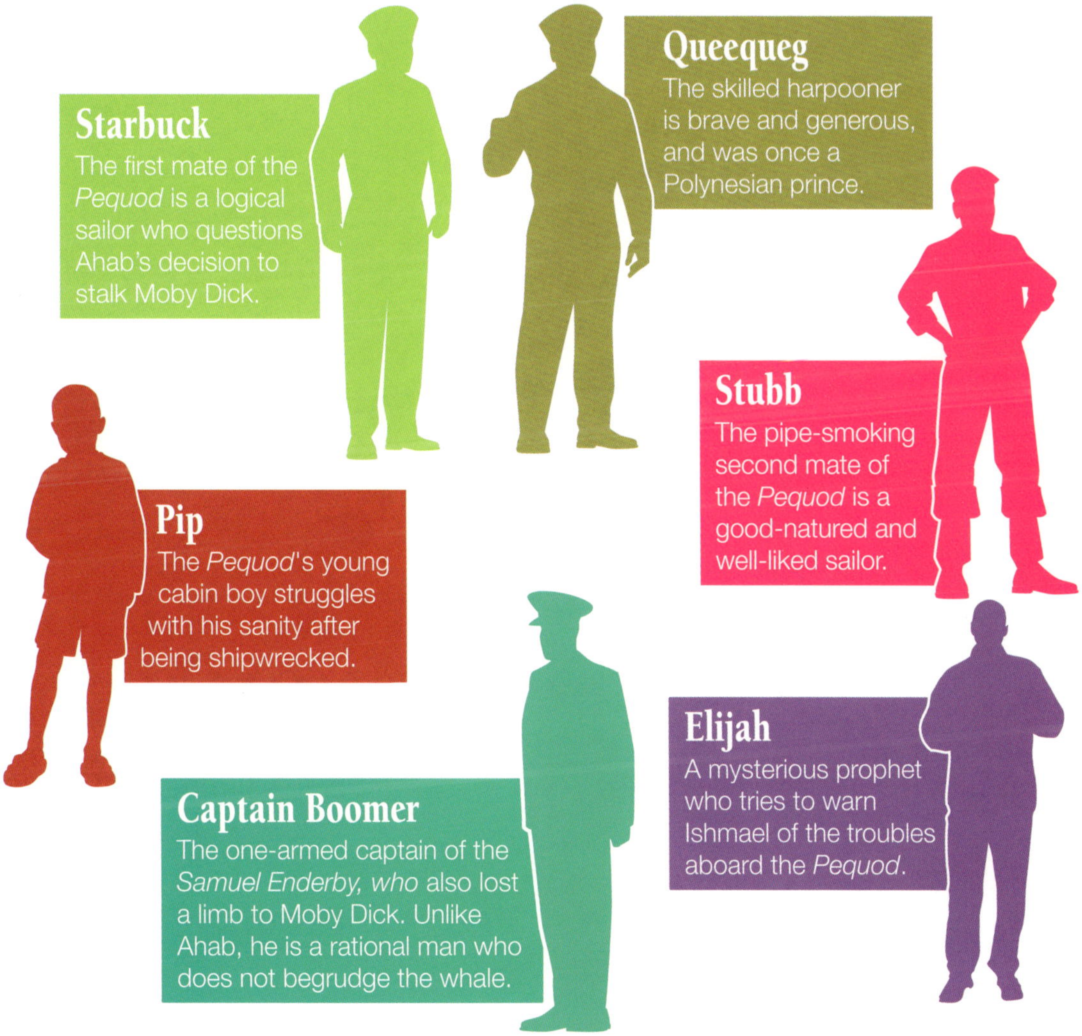

Starbuck
The first mate of the *Pequod* is a logical sailor who questions Ahab's decision to stalk Moby Dick.

Queequeg
The skilled harpooner is brave and generous, and was once a Polynesian prince.

Stubb
The pipe-smoking second mate of the *Pequod* is a good-natured and well-liked sailor.

Pip
The *Pequod*'s young cabin boy struggles with his sanity after being shipwrecked.

Elijah
A mysterious prophet who tries to warn Ishmael of the troubles aboard the *Pequod*.

Captain Boomer
The one-armed captain of the *Samuel Enderby, who* also lost a limb to Moby Dick. Unlike Ahab, he is a rational man who does not begrudge the whale.

TEACHER NOTES

Video

Ahab and Moby Dick
Assess the performances and characterization of Herman Melville's characters as they are portrayed in the 1956 film adaptation of the novel.

1. What aspects of the actors' performances are most effective in the portrayal of the characters as they appear in the novel? Which aspects seem inconsistent or ineffective?
2. What elements would make the film portrayal of the characters more consistent with those in the novel? What kinds of challenges might writers and directors face when adapting a novel such as *Moby Dick?* Provide reasons for your opinions.

More

Character Development in *Moby Dick*
Analyze the characters in *Moby Dick* using the descriptions on the character map and excerpts from each character. Then, choose a character and answer the following questions.

1. Which of the writer's techniques are most effective at revealing this character's traits? Why?
2. In what ways is the characterization of this character ineffective? What could be done to improve this character's function in the novel? Defend your ideas with evidence.

EXTENSION ACTIVITY

Creating a Literary Device Analysis Booklet

Students will analyze the author's use of a literary device in the novel, and create a booklet to present this analysis. An exemplary literary device analysis booklet will meet the following criteria.

- Defines the chosen literary device accurately and in detail
- Places the definition of the literary device at the beginning of the booklet
- Provides strong, specific examples of how this literary device is used in the novel
- Describes examples in detail, with quotations properly integrated
- Includes thorough analysis of the use, purpose, and effectiveness of each example of how the chosen literary device is used in the novel
- Arranges all pages logically
- Examples are organized chronologically
- Provides no more than one example and its analysis per page
- Creates a neat, well-organized, and attractive booklet
- Booklet is colorful and displays the student's creativity
- Uses illustrations to represent the chosen literary device and the examples of how it is used in the novel

The Art of Storytelling

A story is narrative, which is a series of events usually arranged in a logical manner for readers and listeners to enjoy. However, writers use a variety of literary tools to make their stories more entertaining, engaging, and lay bare deeper truths. Herman Melville used a host of literary devices to tell the story of *Moby Dick*. Structure, plot, writing style, and a variety of literary techniques helped Melville convey the message he wanted his readers to understand.

Structure of a Narrative

Each narrative, including *Moby Dick*, has a certain structure. The most common narrative structure used in literature is called dramatic structure, or Freytag's Pyramid. Dramatic structure consists of five main components, all of which appear in *Moby Dick*.

Freytag's Pyramid

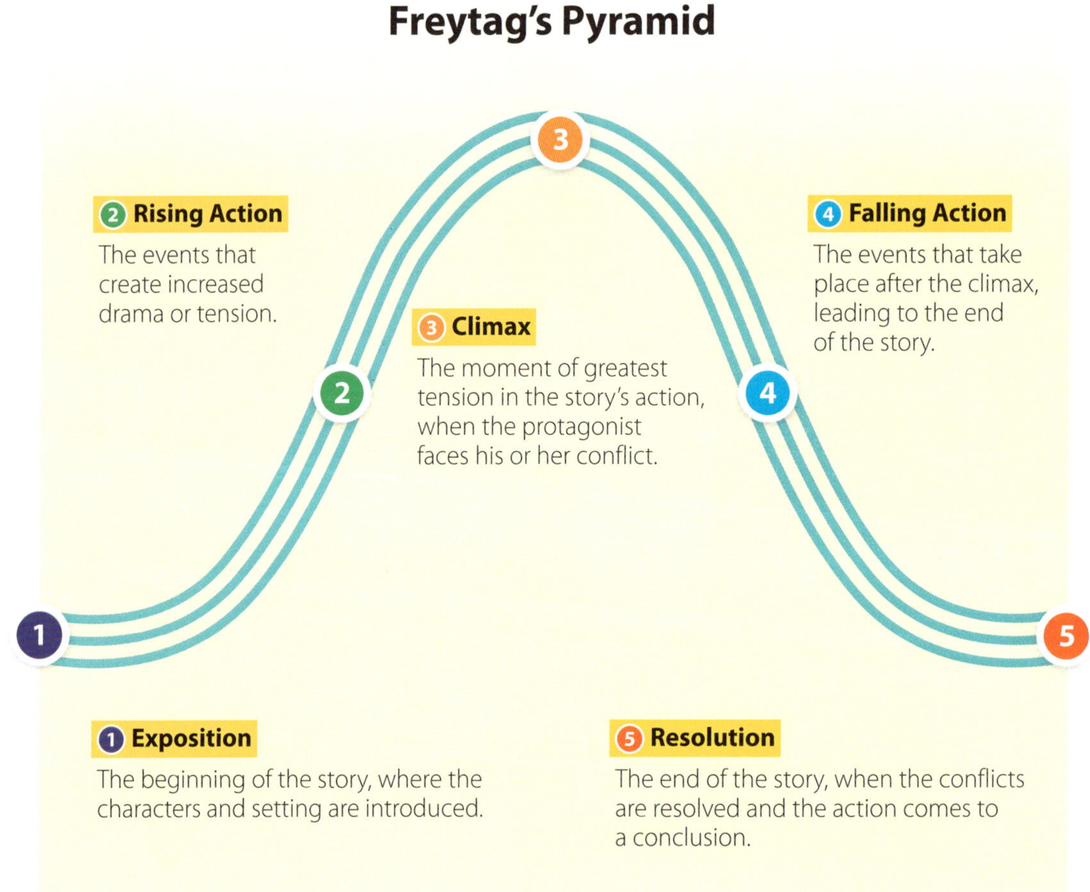

Plot

Central to every narrative is the plot, which is a series of actions that moves the story forward. The plotline is the order in which the events, or plot points, take place. The writer uses each of these plot points, building on one another and organizing them in a coherent fashion. Like a set of falling dominoes, each event causes the next event to happen, which bolsters the narrative.

Plot Points in Chapter 3 of *Moby Dick*

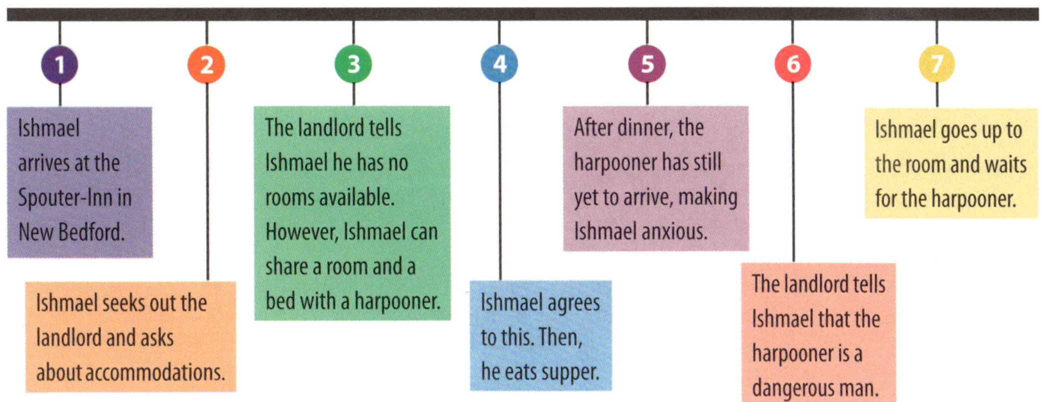

Literary Devices

A literary device is any feature of literature that can be identified, studied, and analyzed. There are two types of literary devices. These are literary elements and literary techniques.

TEACHER NOTES

Weblink

Herman Melville on Writing and His Daily Routine

Examine the blog post discussing Melville's writing habits and daily routine.

1. Can you imagine work such as *Moby Dick* arising from a writer with Melville's daily routine and writing habits? What about it seems sufficient? Does anything about his routine seem inefficient? Justify your responses.
2. What reasons might Melville have for believing "a book in a man's brain is better off than a book bound in calf"? What is Melville suggesting about transmuting ideas to the page?

More

Examples of Literary Techniques from the Novel

Analyze the author's use of literary techniques and how they contribute to the narrative of *Moby Dick*.

1. Choose one literary technique used in the novel. In what particular way did the author use this literary technique? How effective was its usage?
2. What arguments can be made for the use of your chosen literary technique in a text? If this technique were overused or underutilized, what effect might it have on an author's work?

Theme in the Novel

The theme of a story is often a general, universal statement about life. This serves as an underlying idea or position in a narrative. Many times, themes are stated outright, but often they are insinuated, allowing readers to make their own judgments.

Theme is not to be confused with the novel's topic. The topic is the novel's overall subject, while a theme makes an observation or statement about the topic. Themes can be expressed through the events, dialogue, or action within a novel, and readers may have to consider many aspects of the narrative to form their opinion of its themes. Interpretations of a novel's themes often vary from reader to reader, and tend to be as individual as the readers themselves.

Major Themes of *Moby Dick*

There is no shortage of themes in *Moby Dick*. Melville's dark and exciting novel raises questions about nature, the limits of human knowledge, and human behavior and interactions. The major themes in *Moby Dick* include friendship and camaraderie, defiance and obsession, and death.

Ishmael

Friendship and Camaraderie

"We had lain thus in bed, chatting and napping at short intervals, and Queequeg now and then affectionately throwing his brown tattooed legs over mine, and then drawing them back; so entirely sociable and free and easy were we; when, at last, by reason of our confabulations, what little nappishness remained in us altogether departed, and we felt like getting up again, though day-break was yet some way down the future."

Ishmael, Chapter 11

TEACHER NOTES

Weblink

The Importance of Theme: Finding Your Story's North Star
Evaluate the article discussing the thematic writing.

1. The writer of the article states that the best themes reflect universal truths about being human. What themes reflect these truths in *Moby Dick*? Why?
2. Which single-word theme is the "North Star" of the novel? Are there any other words you would use to thematically summarize the novel? Provide evidence justifying your selections.

Starbuck

Defiance and Obsession

"Vengeance on a dumb brute!" cried Starbuck, "that simply smote thee from blindest instinct! Madness! To be enraged with a dumb thing, Captain Ahab, seems blasphemous."

Starbuck, Chapter, 36

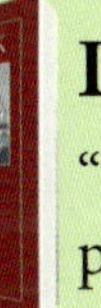

Death

"Ye've shipped, have ye? Names down on the papers? Well, well, what's signed, is signed; and what's to be, will be; and then again, perhaps it won't be, after all. Anyhow, it's all fixed and arranged a'ready; and some sailors or other must go with him, I suppose; as well these as any other men, God pity 'em! Morning to ye, shipmates, morning; the ineffable heavens bless ye; I'm sorry I stopped ye."

Elijah, Chapter 19

Elijah

More

Major and Secondary Themes
Analyze the author's development of themes over the course of the novel.

1. Choose a secondary theme from this spread and analyze its appearances in the novel. How does this theme first emerge? Which is the most poignant example of this theme in the novel?
2. What particular commentary might the author be making about life as a result of this theme's presence in the text? Explain and defend your ideas.
3. Choose a major theme presented on pages 16–17. In what ways does your chosen secondary theme relate to this major theme? Does it deepen or detract from the major theme? How or in what way?

Secondary Themes

Secondary themes do not play as large a role in a narrative, but they add important context. This allows for the narrative to become deeper and more complex. In *Moby Dick*, examples of secondary themes include revenge, duty, the **exploitative** nature of whaling, the science of whales, and the limits of human knowledge.

EXTENSION ACTIVITY

Creating a Symbolism Poster

Students will choose one of the other symbols listed on page 19 and analyze its role in the novel. They will then create a poster to present their analysis. An exemplary symbolism poster will meet the following criteria.

- Presents a clear purpose that is conveyed throughout the poster
- Shows an understanding of the concept of symbolism and the role it plays in the novel
- Provides an in-depth analysis of what the symbol represents
- Discusses the role the symbol plays in the novel
- Clearly indicates where the symbol appears in the novel
- Uses specific, detailed examples from the text to support the analysis
- Makes clear connections to the text
- Properly integrates all quotations
- Organizes the information in a logical, easy-to-read manner
- Includes high-quality graphics that relate to the symbol and effectively enhance understanding of the topic
- Features clear and concise writing
- Uses correct spelling, grammar, and punctuation
- Clearly labels items of importance
- Headings and subheadings are clear and easy to read
- Uses layout to creatively enhances the information
- Creates a poster that is attractive in terms of layout, design, and organization
- Shows a strong effort by the student

Symbolism in the Novel

Symbolism is a literary device used by writers to help convey and intensify a work's themes. A symbol is often a physical object to which a writer imparts a deeper meaning. In some cases, the title of the novel will provide insight into a major symbol. Writers use symbols to convey how they feel about specific events, ideas, and concepts. By identifying and analyzing the symbols a writer uses, the reader can gain a deeper understanding of the story.

The White Whale as a Symbol

The White Whale

"He's welcome to the arm he has, since I can't help it, and didn't know him then; but not to another one. No more White Whales for me; I've lowered for him once, and that has satisfied me."

Captain Boomer, Chapter 100

Many novels have more than one symbol. While *Moby Dick* features a number of symbols, none loom quite as large as the White Whale. For Captain Ahab, Moby Dick is a symbol of evil who seeks to cause death and destruction. For Starbuck, the White Whale is just a whale, which is why he opposes Ahab for chasing an animal out of revenge. The captain of the *Samuel Enderby*, who lost an arm to Moby Dick, sees this whale as a source of rich spermaceti. For others, the White Whale is a myth, a sea **wraith** that does not exist and only lives in the minds of men. Yet there are those who believe the White Whale is a symbol of immortality.

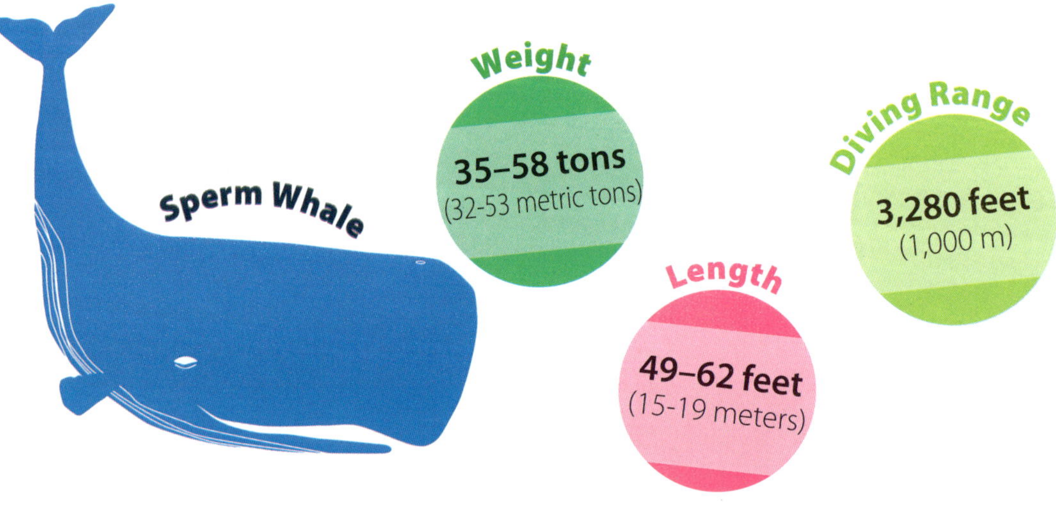

What Does the White Whale Symbolize for These Characters?

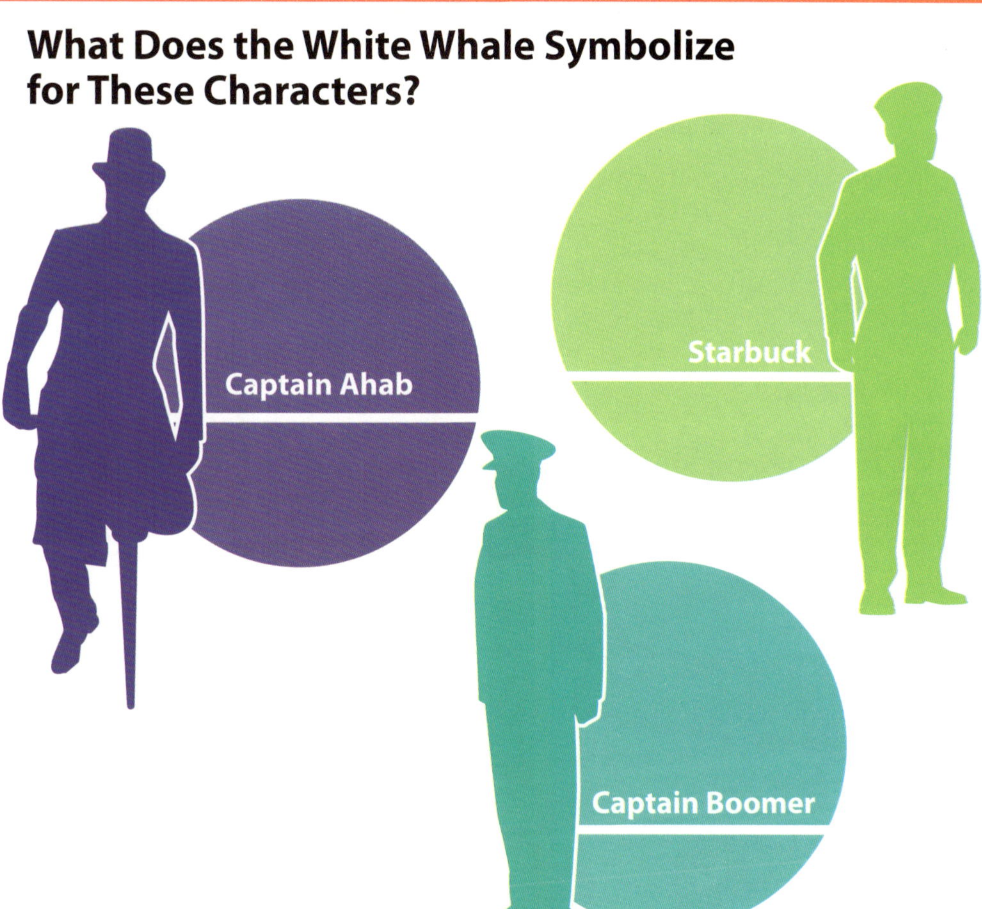

Other Symbols in the Novel

The Pulpit

Early in the novel, readers are introduced to the Whaleman's Chapel, a place where life, death, and whaling merge. Ishmael is taken by the symbolism of the church's pulpit, which is central to the church. It is shaped like the prow of a ship, and Father Mapple is most certainly the captain of that ship. He climbs a rope ladder to the pulpit much as a sailor would climb up to the main mast.

Queequeg's Coffin

Queequeg's canoe-shaped coffin symbolizes his impending death and homesickness for the island where he once lived. Many seafaring cultures throughout history have sent corpses adrift in coffin-like boats. Queequeg's coffin is not just a symbol of death and nostalgia, but of renewal. When Queequeg decides he does not want to die, his coffin becomes a symbol of hope, and later a practical means of saving a life.

TEACHER NOTES

More

What Does the White Whale Symbolize?

Assess the author's use of symbolism in the novel.

1. Choose a character from the chart and analyze what the symbol of the White Whale represents to him. For which character is this symbol the most poignant in the novel? For which character is the symbol least poignant? Argue your opinions with clear reasons.
2. How is this symbol used or reflected in the novel's themes? Illustrate the ways in which the author's use of language deepens or weakens the meaning of the White Whale as a symbol. Explain and defend your ideas.

Weblink

The Complete Guide to Symbolism

Examine the blog post discussing the usage of symbolism in literature.

1. Contrast and compare examples of analytical descriptions of feelings and sensory descriptions using symbolism from the novel. Which kind is more effective in the novel? Provide reasons for your ideas.
2. Should analytical descriptions play a considerable role in the language of a novel? Why or why not?

EXTENSION ACTIVITY

Analyzing Bias in a Document

Students will analyze the bias that exists in a document from a different historical time and place, and how that bias shapes the opinions presented in the document. An exemplary analysis of bias in a document will meet the following criteria.

- Identifies the main points presented in the document
- Offers an in-depth interpretation of the document
- Differentiates between facts and opinions
- Identifies the writer
- Presents information about the writer
- Assesses the writer's reliability
- Determines the goals for the document
- Considers and assesses the writer's perspective
- Determines the writer's intended audience
- Identifies when and where the document was written
- Describes the historical context for the time and place in which the document was created, and analyzes how this context might have shaped the opinions expressed in the document
- Infers political or societal influences that may have shaped the opinions presented in the document
- Determines whether the writer had first-hand knowledge of the topic or event, or whether they are reporting as a secondary source
- Determines the document's bias
- Infers what interests the writer might have had that led them to create this document
- Explores other sources related to the topic of the document

The Use of Language

Like a painter who uses various colors, techniques, and brushes to create a work of art, a writer uses words and language to paint a picture. In *Moby Dick*, Herman Melville uses different parts of speech, particularly metaphors and similes, to paint a portrait of all characters and themes, including the White Whale. He also introduces the reader to a whaler's world by using words specifically relating to sailing and hunting whales. Here are some nautical and whaling terms used in *Moby Dick*.

Metaphors and Similes

A metaphor is a figure of speech in which a writer compares two different things without using a word of comparison. Writers use metaphors to enrich their prose. Similes are figures of speech that compare the similarities between two different objects. Unlike a metaphor, however, similes compare things by using words such as "like" or "as." When using a simile, the writer is making a direct comparison. These comparisons are used throughout Melville's narrative. Here are some examples of similes used in *Moby Dick*.

Examples of Similes in *Moby Dick*

"Here, tossed about the sea, the beginner feels about as cozy as he would standing on a bull's horn."

"With the wondrous sight of the ivory *Pequod* bearing down upon her boats with outstretched sails, like a wild hen after her screaming brood—all this was thrilling."

"The waters flashed for an instant like heaps of fountains, then brokenly sank in a shower of flakes, leaving the circling surface creamed like new milk round the marble trunk of the whale."

"Ahab and his men struggled out from under it like seals from a seaside cave."

"Moby Dick had reaped away Ahab's leg, as a mower a blade of grass in the field."

"'The next instant, in a jiff, I was blind as a bat—both eyes out,' said the one-armed commander."

"For three minutes or more he was seen swimming like a dog, throwing his long arms straight out before him, and by turns revealing his brawny shoulders through the freezing foam. I looked at the grand and glorious fellow, but saw no one to be saved."

"The acute policy dictating these movements was sufficiently vindicated at daybreak, by the sight of a long sleek on the sea directly and lengthwise ahead, smooth as oil, and resembling in the pleated watery wrinkles bordering it, the polished metallic-like marks of some swift tide-rip, at the mouth of a deep, rapid stream."

TEACHER NOTES

Document

A Reading of the "The Maldive Shark" by Herman Melville
Read the poem by Herman Melville and its analysis by Christopher Nield as published in *The Epoch Times*.

1. Compare and contrast Melville's use of language for his descriptions of the Maldive shark and Moby Dick. How are they similar? In what ways do they differ? What reasons might there be for these similarities and differences?
2. How different is Melville's tone in the poem and his tone in the novel? Does he seem to feel differently about the two sea creatures? Why might this be?

Weblink

Herman Melville's Moby-Dick-tionaries
Examine the blog post on the Oxford Dictionaries website discussing Melville's use of language in *Moby Dick*.

1. What reasons might Melville have for including the name for *whale* in 13 languages? What political statement could Melville be making by using a blend of American and English etymologies for *whale*?
2. Is the statement, "Moby Dick is effectively an encyclopedia or dictionary of whales and whaling," an accurate one? Justify your position.
3. What might be discovered about Melville by examining Ishmael's thoughts on writing, language, and words?

EXTENSION ACTIVITY

Writing a Book Review

Students will write a book review of the novel. An exemplary book review will meet the following criteria.

- Grabs the reader's attention with a creative headline
- Begins with an engaging lead to pull the reader into the article
- Introduces the title of the novel, the author, and the genre
- Provides a brief plot description that does not give away the entire story, and makes the reader want to learn more about the novel
- Supports arguments about the novel with accurate and detailed information
- Organizes the review and its arguments in a concise, clear, and logical manner
- Fits the format and style of a book review
- Follows the conventions of print or online journalism
- Demonstrates creativity in their approach
- Writes with a unique, engaging voice and perspective
- Provides fresh insight into the novel
- Provides an honest, authentic opinion on the novel
- Gives a clear recommendation on the novel, backed up by specific textual evidence
- Uses correct spelling, grammar, and punctuation

Impact of the Novel at the Time of Publishing

When it was first published in 1851, *Moby Dick* was considered a commercial failure and received poor reviews. This negative reception prompted Herman Melville to give up his writing career for a time. It would be many years before Melville's epic novel would start to be thought of as one of the greatest American novels ever written.

Publishing Issues

When *Moby Dick* was first published, Melville's British publisher changed the title to *The Whale*. The novel's binding featured images of right whales, but Moby Dick was a sperm whale. The publisher also edited the manuscript without Melville's approval, removing sections he considered vulgar. Melville's epilogue was also cut from this version, leaving British readers wondering whether Ishmael had survived.

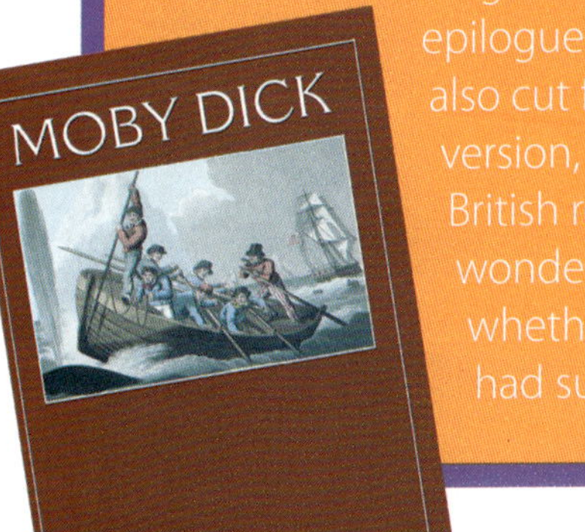

Critical Failure

An early review published in the *London Spectator* in October 1851 heavily critiqued *Moby Dick* for its use of a first-person narrator, stating the novel "... repels the reader instead of attracting him." That same year, a review in the *London Examiner* expressed disappointment in Melville, stating, "We cannot say that we recognize in this writer any advance on the admirable qualities displayed in his earlier books..."

Writing Process

Herman Melville wrote *Moby Dick* in the study of his Massachusetts farmhouse, starting each morning and often working past four o'clock in the afternoon without stopping to eat. He drew on his own experiences as a merchant sailor and whaler, and studied the science of whales to ensure his manuscript included all the latest information about the animals. As he wrote, Melville also read the works of many great authors, including William Shakespeare.

A Writer No More

Melville was disheartened by the failure of his novel. In the years that followed, he became a writer without a story. Melville's professional life as a novelist was essentially over, forcing him to take a job as a customs inspector in New York City. In 1885, Melville's wife received a small inheritance, which allowed him to retire from his customs position. After several years, he put pen to paper again, and wrote what many consider to be one of the greatest novellas in American literature, *Billy Budd*.

Adaptation and Inspiration

The first film based on *Moby Dick* was *The Sea Beast*. This 1926 film starred John Barrymore and was a total departure from Melville's novel, as Ahab kills the whale and finds love. *The Wrath of Khan*, a *Star Trek* film released in 1982, featured a maniacal character named Khan Noonien Singh that seemed to be inspired by Ahab. One of Ahab's most memorable lines from *Moby Dick* is even adapted for the *Star Trek* universe. "I shall have him!" Khan says. "I'll chase him 'round the moons of Nibia and 'round the Antares Maelstrom and 'round perdition's flames before I give him up!"

TEACHER NOTES

Weblink

"It Repels the Reader": Tech Glitches Led *Moby Dick's* First Critics to Pan It

Examine the article discussing the issues that caused the launch of *Moby Dick* to flounder.

1. What reasons might a critic have for attacking Melville's use of first-person narrative? Are these reasons valid? Why or why not?
2. After reading the article, does the headline seem accurate? Was it truly "technical glitches" that caused *Moby Dick*'s initially lukewarm reception?

Video

***The Sea Beast* (1926)**

Compare and contrast a clip from the 1926 film *The Sea Beast*, an adaptation of *Moby Dick*, to the original novel.

1. Think about the cinematography, pacing, action, and content contained in the clip from the film adaptation. Based on the clip, how faithful is the film to the tone and content of the novel? Are there aspects that seem inconsistent or ineffective? Defend your ideas with well-reasoned evidence.
2. For what reasons is silent film a strong medium for an adaptation of *Moby Dick*? How might this medium be lacking when it comes to depicting the novel's events?

EXTENSION ACTIVITY

Analyzing a Song

Students will record or view the lyrics of a song relating to a historic event or topic, and write an analysis of what the song means. An exemplary song analysis will meet the following criteria.

- Chooses an appropriate, relevant song for analysis
- Describes why the specific song was chosen
- Identifies where and when the song was first written
- Identifies the composer of the song
- Provides a copy of the song and its lyrics
- Links the composition of the song to its content
- Researches the cultural and historical context of the song
- Describes who the song is targeted at and why
- Expresses the emotional and intellectual impact of the song
- Examines literary devices used in the song
- Performs an in-depth analysis of any themes found in the song
- Interprets the literal and figurative meaning of the lyrics
- Organizes the analysis in a logical, effective manner
- Cites all sources used in the analysis
- Uses correct spelling, grammar, and punctuation

Impact of the Novel Now

Despite its initial failure, *Moby Dick* resurfaced in the early 1900s and found a new audience. Critics and readers took another look at Melville's tome and decided that it was one of the greatest American novels. In 2002, *Moby Dick* was ranked one of the 100 best books of all time by a panel of 100 international authors. Throughout the years, *Moby Dick* has influenced American culture in several ways. Some universities now devote entire semesters to digging into the novel's many themes and complex characters.

Only **500 copies** of *Moby Dick* ***were initially printed in Great Britain.***

In the ***United States***, only **2,915 copies** of the novel's first edition were ***printed***.

In 2010, a first edition of ***Moby Dick*** sold at auction for **$28,900**.

A New Film Adaptation

In 1956, Hollywood producer John Huston and writer Ray Bradbury teamed up to bring *Moby Dick* to the screen. During the development process, Bradbury spent months agonizing over the adaptation of the weighty novel, which was to be **truncated** to a two-hour movie. As Bradbury recalls in *John Huston: A Biography*, he "got out of bed one morning in London, looked in the mirror, and said, 'I'm Herman Melville!'" Bradbury claims to have then been possessed by the spirit of Melville. Working at a furious clip, he rewrote large portions of the screenplay, completing his work in just eight hours.

Influencing Music

Melville's story has inspired a number of musicians. In 1969, the rock group Led Zeppelin recorded a song, "Moby Dick," featuring a lengthy instrumental drum solo by Jon Bonham. During live performances, Bonham's solo could last for 30 minutes. Some critics saw this as Bonham turning himself into Ahab by trying to achieve the perfect rhythm. Other music inspired by *Moby Dick* includes a song by rapper MC Lars called "Ahab," and an opera adapted by composer Jack Heggie.

The Moby Dick Marathon

Every year, the New Bedford Whaling Museum in New Bedford, Massachusetts, celebrates Melville's classic with a 25-hour non-stop public reading of *Moby Dick*. New Bedford plays a small role in the novel, as it is the place where Ishmael and Queequeg first meet and become friends. More than 150 readers generally participate in the annual event.

EXPLORING THE ORIGINS OF MOBY DICK

In 2000, American author Nathaniel Philbrick published *In the Heart of the Sea*, which explores the haunting shipwreck that inspired Melville to write *Moby Dick*. A film adaptation of Philbrick's book was released in 2015. The film tells the true story of the shipwreck and includes a fictionalized account of Herman Melville hearing this story from the last surviving member of the *Essex*.

TEACHER NOTES

Video

Led Zeppelin – "Moby Dick"
View and analyze a portion of Jon Bonham's drum solo from a live performance of Led Zeppelin's song, "Moby Dick."

1. Are the critics' comparisons of Jon Bonham's performance to Ahab apt? Why or why not?
2. Which aspects of Bonham's performance are most effective at evoking the themes and feelings present in the novel? Explain your opinions.

Weblink

Review: "In the Heart of the Sea," It's Man vs. Leviathan
Analyze the review of the 2015 film adaptation of *In the Heart of the Sea*, as published in *The New York Times*.

1. What conflicts of interest might Hollywood filmmakers face when trying to accurately depict the tone of a nineteenth-century catastrophe at sea? How might the film suffer or succeed as a result of these challenges?
2. The critic notes that the overall message of the film seems to be that domination of nature is not a good thing. How consistent is this with Melville's message? What reasons could there be for any differences between the messages of the two works? Explain and defend your answers with well-reasoned evidence.

EXTENSION ACTIVITY

Creating a Timeline

Students will explore a topic related to the novel and create a timeline to present their research on historical events connected to this topic. An exemplary timeline will meet the following criteria.

- Includes the most significant events pertaining to the topic to be compared and analyzed
- Includes interesting events
- Uses accurate information for all events, including date, location, and major details
- Orders the events in a chronological sequence
- Describes each event with accurate, vivid, and specific details
- Presents the topic from three or more perspectives
- Inspires the reader to ask thoughtful questions regarding the events and perspectives presented in the timeline
- Uses correct spelling, grammar, and punctuation
- Presents the timeline in a visually attractive and striking manner
- Presents the timeline in a neat, organized manner that is logical and easy to follow
- Uses creativity to present the timeline in an engaging manner
- Effectively communicates the historical information relating to the topic
- Supports each event with reliable sources
- Expresses a clear purpose for creating the timeline
- Enhances the reader's understanding of the topic
- Includes a correctly formatted bibliography of all sources used to create the timeline

Perspectives on the Outcomes of Obsession

In the years prior to the publication of *Moby Dick*, industrialism in the United States had fueled an obsession with wealth and power. In the 1840s and 1850s, the country was growing in terms of wealth and geographical size. Like a possessed Ahab, Americans were caught up in a concept called Manifest Destiny. This was the idea that the United States was destined to stretch from one coast to another. However, the cost of America's obsession with Manifest Destiny came at the expense of others.

Timeline of American Expansion in the 1800s

1830s – 1840s

May 28, 1830 President Andrew Jackson signs the Indian Removal Act, which exchanges Native American land in the East for land west of the Mississippi River. The law would decimate many Native American groups in the coming years.

1831 The government forcibly removes the Choctaw nation from its ancestral lands. The removal of the Seminoles from Florida follows in 1832 and the Creek from Alabama in 1834.

1837 By the end of the year, the U.S. government has removed 46,000 Native Americans in the East, opening 25 million acres (10.1 million hectares) of land for white, pro-slavery settlers.

1838–1839 The "Trail of Tears" begins as the U.S. government forces the Cherokee to give up their lands in Georgia and North Carolina. Out of 15,000 people making their way to Oklahoma, about 4,000 die.

1840 William Lloyd Garrison and others walk out of an anti-slavery convention in London when women abolitionists are refused seats.

1845 John L. O'Sullivan writes of "the fulfillment of our manifest destiny to overspread the continent..." He does not realize the power of his words or how they will be interpreted by some as a call for aggression.

May 13, 1846 Congress declares war on Mexico, marking the beginning of the Mexican-American War.

In the 1840s, the United States went to war with Mexico over contested territories. It also began conflicts with many Native American groups over their ancestral homes. African American and Indigenous populations were enslaved to drive profits and industrial growth in the southern states. Echoes of this era can be seen throughout Melville's writing in *Moby Dick*. The *Pequod*'s owners, Peleg and Bildad, have no qualms about exploiting the whalemen aboard the ship for financial gain. Ahab's singular focus causes the suffering of his crew, the destruction of the *Pequod*, and ultimately, the loss of his very life.

1840s – 1850s

February 2, 1848 The Mexican-American War officially ends with the signing of the Treaty of Guadalupe Hidalgo. Mexico cedes more than 525,000 square miles (1.36 million square kilometers) of territory in the west and southwest to the United States.

1849 Harriet Tubman escapes from slavery and becomes a conductor on the Underground Railroad. Some experts estimate that between 40,000 and 100,000 slaves escape from the South to the North.

September 18, 1850 Congress passes the Fugitive Slave Act, mandating the return of runaway slaves in the North back to the South.

May 30, 1854 Congress passes the Kansas-Nebraska Act, which allows those living in the western territories to decide for themselves whether they should join the Union as slave or free states. The idea soon ignites violence in many territories.

1854–1855 Pro-slavery and free-state settlers flood into Kansas, sparking violence as both sides vie for control.

May 21, 1856 Armed ruffians loot the town of Lawrence, Kansas. Days later, in response to the violence, abolitionist John Brown kills five pro-slavery settlers along Pottawatomie Creek.

TEACHER NOTES

Transparency–Timeline

American Expansion in the 1800s Timeline

Examine the historical and cultural, contexts shown on timeline. Then, contrast and correlate its elements with the themes and events presented in *Moby Dick*.

1. In what ways can historical events, culture, and social mores influence a population's perspective on the outcomes of obsessive behavior? How might these elements have shaped the way a reader in the 1850s interpreted the novel?
2. How might the era in which Herman Melville wrote *Moby Dick* have influenced the novel's themes and settings? Where in the novel is this most evident? Explain your reasoning.
3. Which current events, changes in laws, new ideas, or political discussions are preventing the kinds of ideas that fueled Manifest Destiny and its outcomes? Which ideas and ideas are still prevailing? Why?
4. How might current events and present perspectives affect the way a reader interprets the novel? Why is it important for readers to understand the era and context in which a novel is written?

EXTENSION ACTIVITY

Writing a Comparative Essay

Students will compare two literary devices used in the novel, and then write a comparative essay based on their analysis. An exemplary comparative essay will meet the following criteria.

- Consists of a one-paragraph introduction, three body paragraphs, and a one-paragraph conclusion
- Introduction includes an engaging lead statement about the topic of the essay, more detailed information about the novel, and a one-sentence thesis that specifically states the essay's argument
- Body paragraphs include a topic sentence that refers to the thesis and how the idea appears in the novel, a supporting sentence that points to this part of the novel, textual evidence of this idea from the novel, and analysis of this evidence
- Body paragraphs end with a transition to the next paragraph
- Conclusion refers to the topic of the essay and the three points presented in the body paragraphs, and restates the thesis
- Provides a thorough analysis of the literary devices in question
- Cites strong and thorough textual evidence to support analysis of what the novel says explicitly
- Presents a clear, specific thesis that indicates a high level of critical engagement
- Organizes ideas in a logical manner
- Communicates arguments in a clear, effective manner
- Properly integrates all quotations
- Correctly cites all sources used
- Correctly formats bibliography

Writing a Comparative Essay

Moby Dick brings together a band of interesting characters, each with his or her own motivations, wishes, and prejudices. Once you have read the novel, write a comparative essay to explore how Melville uses two literary devices to move the novel forward. This could be a comparison of characters, themes, symbols, or settings. To write a comparative essay, you will need to formulate an argument. Your argument should clearly state how you feel your compared elements are similar or different. Support your argument with sufficient evidence from the novel and valid reasoning.

How to Analyze and Compare Characters

Use the chart to guide your comparison of two characters in *Moby Dick*.

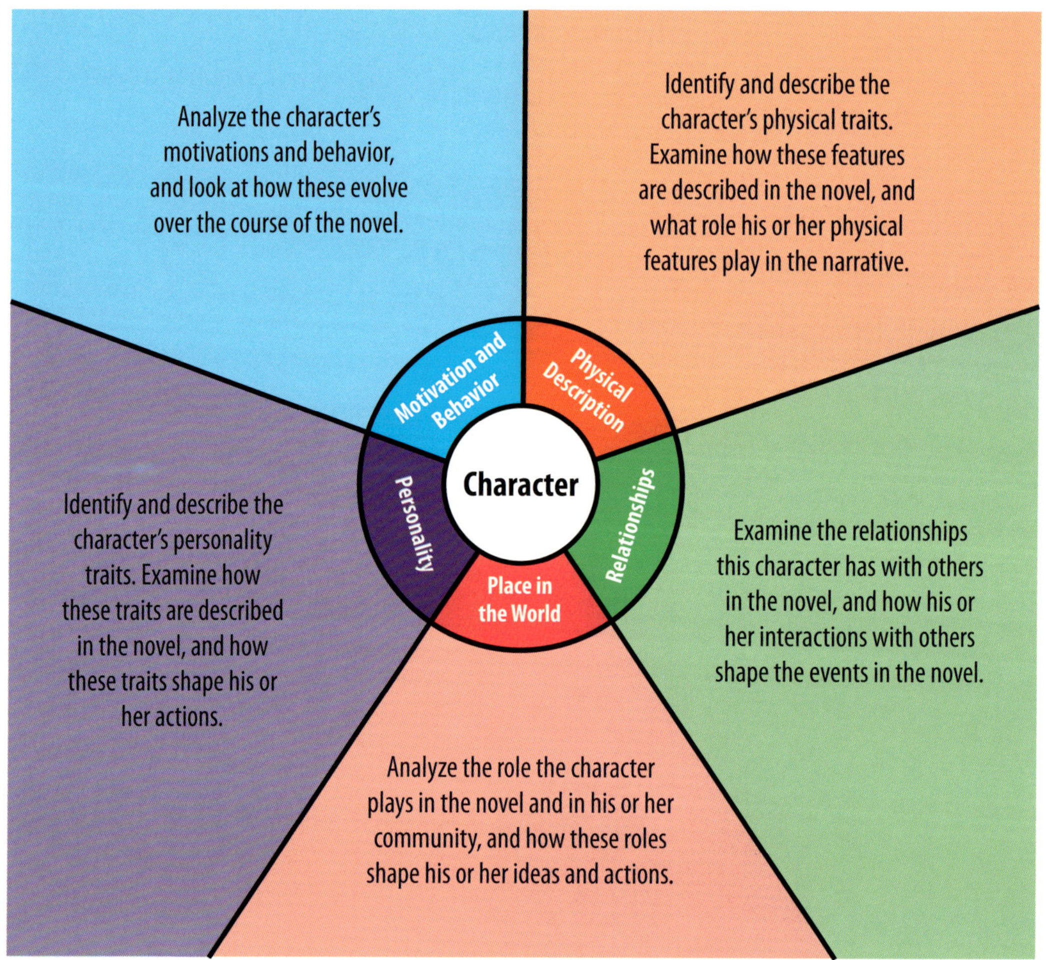

TEACHER NOTES

Comparing Captain Ahab and Ishmael

Captain Ahab

Personality
- Dour
- Egomaniac
- Dictatorial
- Deranged
- Demagogue
- Overconfident
- Believes himself to be God-like

Place in the World
- Leads his crew on a vengeful quest
- Chooses to destroy "evil" despite dangers to himself or to others
- His rank as captain gives him total authority over the crew

Motivation and Behavior
- Driven by his hatred of the White Whale
- Single-minded in his unwavering quest
- Moby Dick propels him to a predetermined end
- Becomes more vengeful as the story unfolds

Physical Description
- Has a peg leg made of whalebone
- Physically imposing
- Described as a broad form made of solid bronze

Relationships
- Married with two children
- Has no friends aboard *Pequod*
- Defies the ship's owners
- Interacts sparingly with the crew
- Manages to sway crew with his fervent zeal

Ishmael

Place in the World
- Is unsure of his place in the world
- A good Christian
- Knows the sea is unforgiving
- Gets aboard the *Pequod* to be part of the sea

Physical Description
- Looks like a seaman
- Young man

Motivation and Behavior
- Optimistic and upbeat as he sets to rid himself of his depression
- Eager to tell the story of Moby Dick, Ahab, and the *Pequod*
- Spares no effort

Relationships
- Comes from an old, established family
- Best friends with Queequeg
- Gets along well with other characters
- Others see him as responsible and modest

Personality
- Says he is "tormented"
- Seeks solace in the sea
- Educated
- Observant
- Provides for himself
- Brave
- Hardworking

Transparency–Chart

Questions for Character Analysis

Analyze how specific character features, such as conflicts, motivations, relationships, place in the world, and personality affect the plot of *Moby Dick*. Cite strong and thorough textual evidence to support your analysis of what the novel says explicitly as well as the inferences you may have drawn from the novel's setting, themes, and symbols.

Quiz Answers

1. B
2. D
3. B
4. B
5. C
6. B
7. C
8. A
9. A
10. A

Key Words

abolitionists: those who wanted to do away with slavery

bankrupt: declared by law unable to pay outstanding debts; something lacking in value

bombastic: given to a manner of verbose, self-important speech verging on pretention

exploitative: taking advantage of a person or situation for personal gain

hubris: exaggerated confidence or pride to the point of conceit

incarnation: a physical form representing something else

lamented: mourned or grieved

maniacal: having the characteristics or behavior of madness

prejudice: a preconceived opinion or idea formed without reason or sufficient knowledge

truncated: shortened or reduced in length by cutting off a portion

wraith: a ghost-like image of someone or something that appears shortly before or after his or her death

Literary Terms

action: everything that occurs in a narrative

antagonist: the character who stands in opposition to the protagonist; in some cases, the antagonist creates or represents the conflict that the protagonist faces

characterization: the act of describing a character through the person's appearance and personality

conflict: a struggle between two or more opposing forces, creating tension that must be resolved

dialogue: the spoken conversations that the characters have with each other

exposition: the beginning of the story, where the characters and setting are introduced

falling action: the events that take place after the climax, leading up to the end of the story

Freytag's Pyramid: a narrative structure consisting of five elements; this includes exposition, rising action, climax, falling action, and resolution

literary elements: components of every literary work

literary techniques: unique structures of a literary work

metaphor: a figure of speech in which a writer compares two different things without using a word of comparison

mood: the overall feeling that the narrative is intended to evoke within the reader

narrative: a logically arranged series of events presented for an audience; a story of sentences

plot: the specific action that propels a story forward

protagonist: the central character in a piece of fiction who must deal with a conflict and often undergoes some type of change as a result

resolution: the end of the story, when the problems are resolved and the action comes to a conclusion

rising action: the events that create increased drama or tension before the story's climax

satire: use of humor, irony, or exaggeration

simile: a figure of speech that compares the similarities between two different objects using words such as "like" or "as"

style: the unique way that writers use language to tell their story. This can include word choice, the use of imagery, and sentence length and organization.

symbolism: a stylistic device using symbols to represent and intensify concepts and ideas

theme: the underlying idea or position of a work that is often a general, universal statement about life

Index

LIGHTBOX

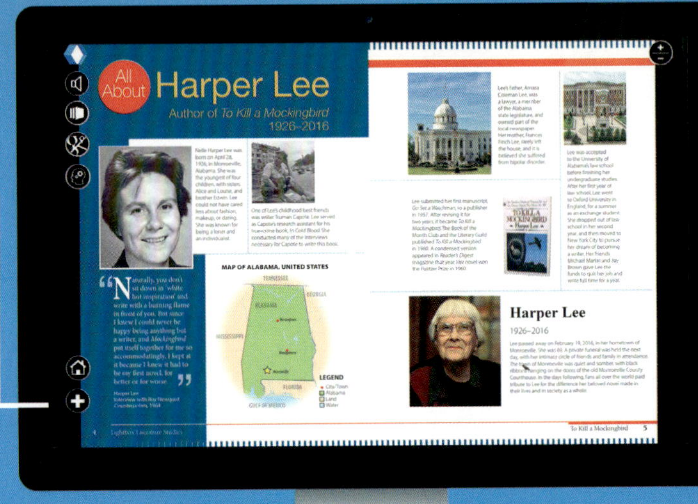

SUPPLEMENTARY RESOURCES

Click on the plus icon found in the bottom left corner of each spread to open additional teacher resources.

- Download and print the book's quizzes and activities
- Access curriculum correlations
- Explore additional web applications that enhance the Lightbox experience

LIGHTBOX DIGITAL TITLES
Packed full of integrated media

VIDEOS

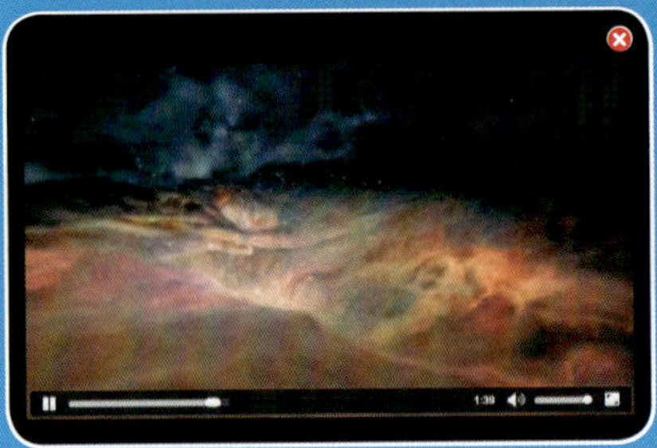

INTERACTIVE MAPS

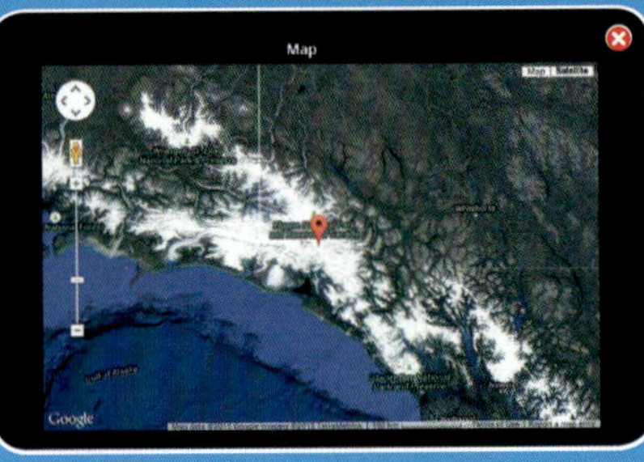

WEBLINKS

SLIDESHOWS

QUIZZES

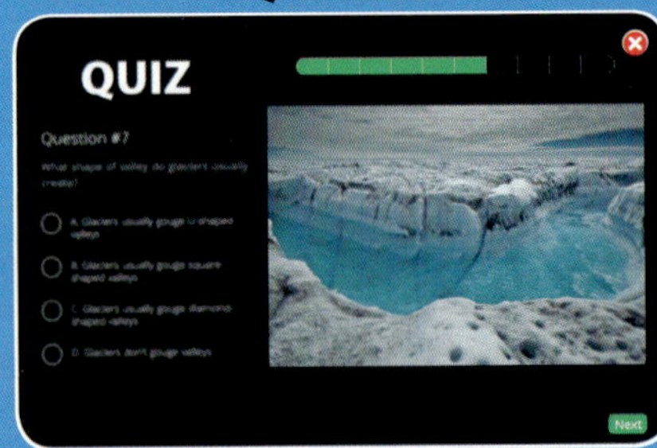

OPTIMIZED FOR
- ✓ TABLETS
- ✓ WHITEBOARDS
- ✓ COMPUTERS
- ✓ AND MUCH MORE!

Published by Smartbook Media Inc.
350 5th Avenue, 59th Floor New York, NY 10118
Website: www.openlightbox.com

062017
042017

Library of Congress Cataloging-in-Publication Data

Names: Perritano, John, author.
Title: Moby Dick / John Perritano.
Description: New York : Smartbook Media Inc., [2018] | Series: Lightbox literature studies | Includes index.
Identifiers: LCCN 2016056510 (print) | LCCN 2017016384 (ebook) | ISBN 9781510520028 (multi-user ebk.) | ISBN 9781510520011 (hard cover : alk. paper)
Subjects: LCSH: Melville, Herman, 1819-1891. Moby Dick--Examinations--Study guides.
Classification: LCC PS2384.M62 (ebook) | LCC PS2384. M62 P477 2018 (print) | DDC 813/.3--dc23
LC record available at https://lccn.loc.gov/2016056510

Printed in Brainerd, Minnesota, United States
1 2 3 4 5 6 7 8 9 0 21 20 19 18 17

Project Coordinator: Jared Siemens
Art Director: Terry Paulhus

Every reasonable effort has been made to trace ownership and to obtain permission to reprint copyright material. The publisher would be pleased to have any errors or omissions brought to its attention so that they may be corrected in subsequent printings. The publisher acknowledges Getty Images, Alamy, Shutterstock, Minden Pictures, and iStock as its primary image suppliers for this title.